ANCIENT INDIAN PHILOSOPHY OF EDUCATION

Dr. N. ANANDAKUMAR
Ph.D., (Microbiology), Ph.D., (Education)
Assistant Professor in Philosophy of Education - Contract Basis
Department of Education
The Gandhigram Rural Institute - Deemed to be University
Gandhigram, Dindigul- Dt. Tamilnadu, India

SHANLAX PUBLICATIONS

Title:	ANCIENT INDIAN PHILOSOPHY OF EDUCATION
Author's Name:	Dr. N. Anandakumar
Published by:	Shanlax Publications, Vasantha Nagar, Madurai - 625003, Tamil Nadu, India
Publisher's Address:	61, 66 T.P.K. Main Road, Vasantha Nagar, Madurai - 625003, Tamil Nadu, India
Printer's Details:	Natarajan Publishing House, 11-A/37, Rajiv Gandhi Nagar, Vengamedu, Karur - 639006. Ph: 9443120955 Email: anandakumarn@yahoo.com
Edition Details (I,II,III):	I
ISBN:	978-93-91373-68-9
Month & Year:	November, 2021
Copyright @	Dr. N. Anandakumar
Pages:	43
Price:	₹195/-

PREFACE

This monograph guides you to understand the basic concept of Ancient Indian Philosophy of Education. It depicts scriptural, sculpture and inscription information based on the author's observation and experiences. It contains an introduction to philosophy of education, Vedic philosophy of education, Buddhism philosophy of education and Jainism philosophy of education. The book primarily prepared forB.Ed., M.Ed., and B.Sc. B.Ed., students.

I specially thank my beloved teachers from Department of Philosophy, Annamalai University, Chidambaram for valuable suggestions for this publication.

Also, my heartfelt thanks to Dr. A. Jahitha Begum, Professor and Head, and Faculty Members from Dept. of Education, The Gandhigram Rural Institute, Gandhigram for encouraging and motivation for this publication.

Dr. N. Anandakumar

CONTENTS

INTRODUCTION TO PHILOSOPHY OF EDUCATION

Nature and Meaning of Philosophy of Education

A philosophy as the most general way of thinking about the meaning of our lives in the World. It reflects deeply on what is true or false, right or wrong and beautiful or ugly. Teachers need to think philosophically about the broad cultural and ethical implications of education. Self-reflection is a way to develop a coherent conceptual framework. It leads to reflective practice in the classroom. The term philosophy has a Greek origin. It can be traced to the Greek philosophia, which made up to two words. Philo means love and Sophia means wisdom. A love of wisdom is the essence of any philosophical investigation. According to Cicero, philosophy is the mother of all arts. It is a true medicine of mind.

The philosophers' attitude is taking universe as a systematic whole. It concerned with ultimate reality. The revelation of some truth by every experiences. Alexander point of view, metaphysics as reality and universe. Immanuel Kant's considered as metaphysical experiences. The proper function of philosophy is a logical analysis of the proposition of science. Philosophy is wisdom, education transmits that wisdom from one generation to the next generation. It represents, a system of thought, whereas, education embraces that thought in the content of instruction. The aim of education is directly related with the aim of life and aim of life is always dependent on the philosophy that prevails. Philosophy determines whether the aim of education should be moral perfection or intellectual development. Determination of curriculum needs the services of philosophy in its entirety. A philosophy is needed to determine the quality and contents of text books.

Plants are shaped by cultivation and men by education. We are born weak, we need strength. We are born totally unprovided, we need aid. Everything we do not have at our birth and which we need when we are grown is given us by education-Jean Jacques Rousseau, Emile, On Philosophy of Education. It is not easy to say, what exactly philosophy is, how to study it, or how to do it. Philosophy is unique. Philosophy in one way ends up touching upon nearly every aspect of human life. Philosophy is so important for all mankind.

Different Areas of Philosophy of Education

There are four major branches of philosophy such as metaphysics, epistemology, axiology and logic.

Metaphysics examines the nature of ultimate reality. What is real and what is not real? Is there a spiritual world existence separate from the material world? Ex. Idealists' reality is non material nature or spiritual terms. It is the study of existence, reality or essence. Its main branches are cosmogony, cosmology, ontology, philosophy of self and eschatology. Cosmogony means study of creation. Ex. Is the world created or is its eternal nature or who created the world? What is the purpose in creation? All these are the problems of cosmogony. Cosmology means, Is the world one ormany. Ontology means ultimate reality. Ex. Is the reality one or is it many. Philosophy of self means philosophical analysis of self or what is self. Eschatology means, discussion of the condition of soul after death.

Epistemology is the most fundamental branch of philosophy. It discusses philosophically truth, falsehood, validity of knowledge and nature of knowledge.

Axiology prescribes values. It is subdivided into ethics and aesthetics. Ethics examines moral and standard of ethical behaviour, whereas, aesthetics addresses values in beauty and art. Teachers, parents and society convey their values to the young by rewarding and reinforcing behaviour that corresponds to their conceptions of what is right, good and beautiful.

Logic examines the rates of inference that use to frame our propositions and arguments. Ex. Deductive logic moves from general statements to particular instances or application.

> "All deciduous trees seasonally drop their leaves;
> The maple tree drops it leaves in the fall;
> The maple is a deciduous tree;"

Inductive logic moves from the particular instance to tentative generalization. Ex. The earth's temperature has been increasing in the last fifty years.

Curriculum and instruction are organized on conceptions of logic. Logic is the study of the principles of right reasoning. Logic is the basic tool that philosophers use to investigate reality.

Every system of education has strong basis of nature of reality, knowledge and values. These are called Sat Chit and Ananda. On the basis of these three philosophical foundations, education has performed. Reality is always existential priority, whereas knowledge is noetic priority. In human consideration, reality is only through knowledge. Hence, epistemic is most fundamental one.

According to John Dewey, whenever philosophy has been taken seriously, it has always been assumed that it signified achieving a wisdom, that would influence the conduct of life. Philosophy is the study of general and fundamental problems concerning matters, such as existence, knowledge, truth, beauty, law, justice, validity, mind and language. Philosophy is rationally thinking of a more or less systematic kind about the general nature of the world.

1. Metaphysics or theory of existence, (The justification of belief).
2. Epistemology or theory of knowledge
3. Conduct of life-Ethics or theory of value

Hence, philosophy is a subject at the core of most humanities courses. It focuses on abstract questions like...

1. Does God exist?
2. Is the world really as it appears to us?
3. How should we live?
4. What is art?
5. Do we have genuine freedom of choice?
6. What is the mind?

The study of philosophy is usually approached in one of two different ways:

1. Systematic method
2. Historical method

To study philosophy, you have to engage in philosophical argument-reasons or evidence leading to a conclusion. Therefore, a philosopher is a wise person who is calm and rational, and someone who lives a life of reason with equability.

Modes of Philosophy of Education

There are three modes of philosophizing as suggested by Kneller (1971).

A. Speculative philosophy: This is the attempt to find a coherence in the whole realm of thought and experience.
B. Prescriptive philosophy: It seeks to discover and to recommend principles for deciding. What actions and qualities are most worthwhile? It examines what we

mean by good and bad, right and wrong, beautiful and ugly.

C. Analytic philosophy: Focuses on words and meaning. It examines concepts or notions. Ex. Cause, equality of opportunity, academic freedom, etc.

Patterns of Philosophy of Education

Soltis (1981) suggests to consider three perspectives of philosophy of education:

1. Personal:

The personal beliefs of every educator in terms of what are sensible, right or good to do in the process of learning form the educator's personal philosophy of education, just like a person's philosophy of life.

2. Public:

Public sense of philosophy of education is connected with public expressions of opinions in matters of education, what the public comes to judge as good and right to be done in education.

3. Professional:

The professional aspect of philosophy of education has to do with accumulated wisdom expressed by educational theorists who have undergone professional training in philosophy.

Teachers Need Philosophy of Education-Why

There are four reasons are given for this necessity.

A. The development of rationality and reasonableness in children.

B. For teachers to be effective in teaching their subjects, they must understand those subjects well. To do this, they will ask fundamental philosophical questions about them.

- What is the nature of the given subject?
- What is its basic structure?
- Its purpose?
- Its value?
- Its methods?

C. Socrates and Plato concepts as beliefs, language, values, indoctrination, open-mindedness, autonomy, freedom, authority, punishment and discipline are crucial to education. They are discussed in philosophy of education.

D. Moral education is an attempt at raising the degree of critical awareness of the ethics of the teaching profession. In the branch of philosophy of education, the teachers in making have the opportunity to study concepts like rights, duties, obligations, virtues and vices. It is hoped that in that way they may grow more morally aware.

Functions of Philosophy of Education

Different schools of thoughts have started with different meta-physical views. For example, a pragmatist or instrumentalist would be a stress upon activity methods, like projects, experiments, problem-solving etc.

Instead like a realist if knowing regarded as outside to be known. Here, education would be regarded as outer reality to the knower. So, learning would be regarded as true and effective through outer reality. Learner would be regarded as a passive instrument, have an empty mind like a tabula rasa. More emphasis would be laid on natural sciences and knowledge of the external world.

As an idealist emphasis would be laid on the constructive activity of the mind, out of what is given in immediate experience. For example, education would be a constant training of body, will and mind. In learning process self-activity, introspection, meditation etc. will acquire prominence. Spiritual education would occupy a place of honor in the curriculum.

Great philosophers of all times have also been Great educators and their philosophy is reflected in their educational systems. So, each one of us has a personal philosophy, which we apply consciously and unconsciously in our daily life. Each philosophy reflects a unique view of what is good and what is important. Philosophy is the system of belief about life. The literal meaning is the love of wisdom. Wisdom does not merely mean knowledge. It is a continuous seeking of insight into basic realities:

1. The physical world
2. Life
3. Mind
4. Society
5. Knowledge
6. Values

Any separation of philosophy and education inhibits frustrates the wisdom. Hence, education needs direction and guidance, which philosophy can provide. Philosophy is not only a professional tool for the educators, but also a way of improving the quality of life. Philosophy deals good life, education achieve those good life. Philosophy is theory and education practical. Rose said, philosophy is contemplative side, whereas education is active side.

VEDIC PHILOSOPHY OF EDUCATION

Introduction to Vedic Philosophy

Vedic philosophy has one of the oldest and longest traditions of philosophical thinking in the World.Vedic period includes Puranas and Darsanas. It comprising, the philosophical system of Nyaya (logic and analytic), Vaisesika (consciousness), Sankhya (matter), Yoga (self-control), Mimamsa (critical investigation of veda) and Vedanta (essence of veda). The ancient Indian school of thought can be broadly categorized in two system:

1. Ashthika
2. Nashthika

Ashthika means those which believe veda called as orthodox. Nashthika means those which do not believe veda called as heterodox. Ex. Charwak, Buddhism and Jainism.Vedic literature is 'Apaurusheya' nature. It means non-human and beginningless origin. Vedic period begun from 1500 BC, whereas Upanishadic period begun from 500 BC.

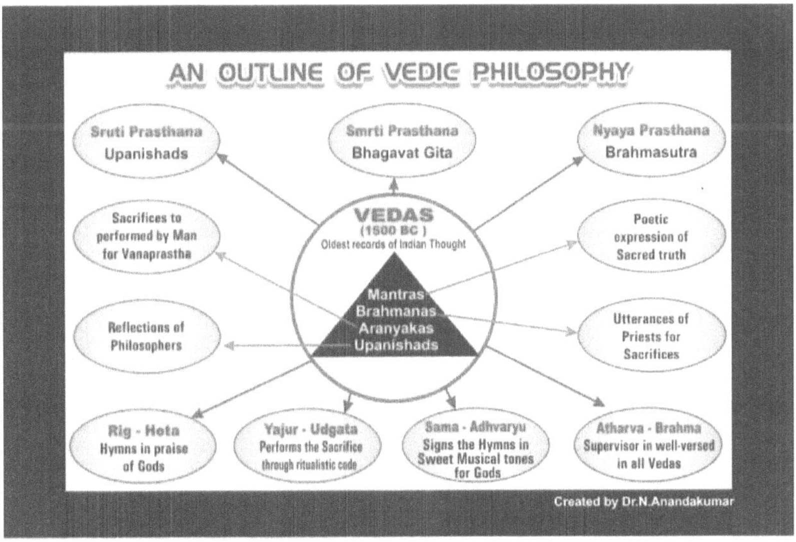

Figure-1 shows an outline of Vedic philosophy

Veda is derived from the root of 'Vid', which mean 'to know'. It acquires the knowledge through the sacred love. There are four Vedas,

1. Rigveda means mantras (Jyana),
2. Samaveda means songs (Bhaki),
3. Yajur means rituals (Karma), and
4. Atharva deals with various sciences.

Besides, Rishi's wrote the Brahmans (Sacrifices for Grihastha) and Aranyakas (Rituals for Vanprasthas) to explain mysterious mantras. The original belief is Monotheism, which means belief in only one God. It was fully developed during the period of Upanishads.

Indian philosophical thoughts have three branches known as Pras-thana-traya.

1. Sruti Prasthana -Upanishads
2. Smrti Prasthana- Bhagavat Gita
3. Nyaya Prasthana- Brahma Sutra

Indian philosophy has been intensely spiritual and need of practical realization of truth. See the reality in you. Indian philosophy traced back Vedas. Hence, Vedas have philosophy, religion, ritual and science. It started from mind of Aryans.

Each Veda is composed of

1. Mantras (Poetic expression of sacred truths)
2. Brahmanas (Utterances of priests for sacrifices)
3. Aranyakas (Sacrifices for vanaprastha)
4. Upanishads (Reflections of philosophers)

Samhitas developed by four priests

1. Hota-Rig (Hymns in Praise of God)
2. Udgata-Sama (Hymns musical tone)
3. Adhvaryu -Yajur (Ritualistic code)
4. Brahma – Atharva (Supervisor)

There has been a gradual development from Mantras to Upanishads. Transition from naturalistic polytheism (fire, wind, sun and anthropomorphic form) through monotheism to monism.

A. Upanishads:

Upanishads explain ultimate reality of the universe. It means sit near by devotedly.

Upa-Near by

Ni-Devotedly

Sad-Sit.

Upanishads is concluding portions of the vedas. Hence called Vedanta. Principal Upanishad is ten.

1. Isa
2. Kena
3. Katha
4. Prashna
5. Mundaka
6. Mandukya
7. Taittiriya
8. Aitareya
9. Chandogya
10. Brah daranyaka

Upanishads have two dimensions: Universe (Brahman) and Man (Atman). Upanishads explained Brahman into two forms:

1. Para Brahman-Sat/Chit/Ananda (Infinite/ No attributes)
2. Apara Brahman (Lower).

A ten thousand years is like few seconds for those who tasted the nectar of para-knowledge, whereas a few seconds is like ten thousand years for those whose aparaknowledge. The principle behind the universe called Brahman is essentially indescribable. Taittiriya Upanishads notes as (yatovachonivartanteaprapyamanasasaha). All elements are born in Brahman and culminate in Brahman. It is ultimate substratum of universe. Brah daranyaka Upanishads suggests netineti. Chandogya Upanishads Brahman is described as Tajjalan (Tat-World arises, Ja-Returns, La-Supported and An-lives). The principle behind the man is termed as Atman. Atman originally meant breath, which its self or soul. Mundaka Upanishads identifies 4 states of consciousness.

1. Wakeful (Jagrat)
2. Dream (Swapna)
3. Deep sleep (Sushupti)
4. Fourth state (Turiya).

The eye, body, mental states and stream of consciousness are all mere instruments of the self. Hence, self is universal, immanent as well as transcendent. The ultimate goal of life according to Upanishad's philosophy is self-realization. Brahdaranyaka suggests three steps for inquiry:

1. Sravana (Listening)
2. Manana (Repeating)
3. Nididhyasana (Absorbing)

Though these steps, a person realizes his self. Subjective side as Atman, objective side as Brahman. Brah daranyaka estimates bliss experience greater than pleasure experience. The fusing of two expressed in many ways Mahavakyas:

1. Tatvamasi (That thou art)
2. AhamBrahmasmi (I am Brahman)
3. Ayam atma Brahma (This self is Brahman)
4. Prajanam Brahma (Consciousness is Brahman)

B. Bhagavat Gita

The Bhagavat Gita is an episode in India's Great epic Mahabharatha. The main story of Mahabharatha is the war between the Kourava and Pandava. Kouravas are hundred sons of Dhritarastra led by the eldest son Duryodhana. Pandava are five sons of Pandu led by the eldest brother Yadhistira. Only an ignorant person would discriminate children as his brother's sons and his own sons. Here the character Dhritarastra is a symbol of ignorance. Krishna and Arjuna are important characters in the Gita. Krishna as knower, whereas Arjuna as seeker. This episode displayed as war of dharmayaddha against adharma.

Gita says that man is a combination of intellect (thinks), emotion (feels) and will. Three paths for man to achieve the ultimate goal of salvation. Gita uses the term 'Yoga' in the sense of union with God. Realization of God is the highest goal.

1. Jnana yoga
2. Bhakthi yoga
3. Karma yoga

Jnana yoga says the five knowledge reduces all our relish and desire to ashes. Even that most sinful man can cross the ocean with knowledge alone.

Bhakthi yoga says the ideal devotee is one who is dedicated to the service of God.

Karma yoga says 'Nishkamakarma' ordinarily all our actions are motivated by some desire for achieving some result (Bhala). For Karma yoga your concern is solely with actions, never with its fruit (Karmaphalatyaga).

1. Desires often misguides us.
2. It makes us deviate from the right path
3. Hence, when desire of result is renounced, we can act with balance of mind.

There are two ideals of life:

1. Pravriti (Performance of Action)
2. Nivriti (Turning away from activities)

Gita synthesizes Pravriti and Nivriti Ex. Perform the assigned action. Gita says that there are two supreme motives:

1. Atma sudhi (Self- purification)
2. Isvara seva (Self- realization)

"Do our duty to the best of our ability without selfishness. It will lead us to Atma sudhi and Isvara seva help us to achieve God realization".

Stitaprajna: It means higher consciousness. Stitaprajna is 'Man of steady wisdom'. He is an ideal yogi. He always performs Karma for Dharma. He is free from ego and motives. He keeps equal distance from the dualities.

1. Pain and pleasures
2. Wishes and frustrations
3. Joy and sorrow
4. Honour and dishonour

He has escaped from the Samsara (Cycle of birth and death). He is a man who embraces peace. The Stitaprajna sees the presence of God not merely in the good and noble, but also in the wicked and ignoble. He is Jivan Mukta (The liberated soul).

C. Brahmasutra

Brahmasutra is an attempt to synthesize the various of the Upanishads. Badarayana initiated in 500BC-200BC. Also known as Vedanta-Sutra. Sutra means aphorism or rules. A number of commentaries written by number of authors.

1. Sankaracharya
2. Ramanujacharya
3. Madhvacharya

Brahmusutra consists of 555 aphorisms, 4 chapters and each chapter being divided 4 sections.

1. Ultimate reality
2. Objections against Vedanta philosophy
3. Emancipation
4. Final Emancipation

Darsanas

Darsana is the term used to describe a 'System Philosophy'. Great sages and their visions are known as Darsanas.

A. Nyaya Philosophy of Education

Nyaya darsana discusses the source of knowledge. It gives more importance to epistemological issues. It is pluralism and logical realism nature. Ultimately, many kinds of substances in the world. It also known as 'Tarkasasthra' or science of reasoning. It is realism, because it accepts the reality of external world. The basic text of Nyaya system is the Nyaya sutra of Gautama. Nyaya system states that whatever exists is knowable. Nyaya there are two types of knowledge.

1. Prama (Valid Knowledge)
2. Aprama (Invalid knowledge)

Ex. A person mistakes a rope for a snake in dimlight, it is Aprama. Later he realizes his mistake in clear light and perceive rope only, it is Prama. Nyaya have four valid sources of knowledge. They are called Pramanas.

1. Pratyaksa (Perception): It is non-erroneous cognition or immediate cognition. There are two types of perception.
    - Ordinary perception Ex. Sense perception
    - Extraordinary perception Ex. Intuitive perception
2. Anumana (Inference): It is normally based on prior perception. There are three inferences. Nyaya concept of inference has some resemblance with Western syllogism
    - Paksa
    - Hetu
    - Sadhya
3. Upamana (Comparison): Ex. A person says that he has seen an animal named Gavaya in forest. You are curious to know about the animal. His response is that Gavaya is a forest cow having resemblance with domestic cow.
4. Sabda (Verbal testimony): Sabda is the testimony of a trustworthy person. Testimony is of two kinds
    - Vedic (Vaidika)
    - Secular (Loukika)

B. Vaisesika Philosophy of Education

Atoms are the basis of the universe. Vaisesika is derived from 'Visesa' which means excellence, distinction or superiority. Vaisesika is interested in 'Metaphysical issues'. Kanada is founder of Vaisesika school. 'Categories Process' is the central concept in Vaisesika metaphysics. The universe is the combination of seven categories:

1. Dravya (Substance)
2. Guna (Quality)
3. Karma (Action)
4. Samanya (General)
5. Visesa (Particular)
6. Samavaya (Inference)
7. Abhava (Non-existence)

Dravya is a 'Principal Category' of Vaisesika system. Ex. All things of the universe are derived from Dravya.

C. Sankhya Philosophy of Education

The sankhya philosophy is dualistic nature.

1. Prakriti (Nature)
    - Sattva (Light)
    - Rajas (Activity)
    - Tamas (Darkness)
2. Purusha (Spirit) Ex. Conscious and eternal

All knowledge is personal and fragmentary. Sensory organs and 'Antahkarana' helps in perception. Sankhya philosophy is the great work of Sage Kapila. Western philosophers have great admiration for this system. Sankhya means number or perfect knowledge (Samyogjnana). Prakriti offers five arguments:

1. All elements of the world are limited and dependent
2. All elements have common characteristics
3. All elements have some potential

4. All elements have some effects
5. All elements have some causes

The earliest text 'Nirisvara Karika' does not discuss existence of God. The entire universe is a system of cause and effect not by God. Realize the self -knowledge and liberate the soul from the body (Prakriti). Education should train the individual to bring out the natural potential. Ex. Prakriti Mahat means 'A Great One'. Intellect is the finest aspect of a human. Education should train the right proportion of 'Gunas'. Knowledge is perception (Valid Perception) or Buddhi, Inference and shabda. Teacher provide guidance to acquire true knowledge to discriminate between

1. Real self
2. Non-real self

D. Yoga Philosophy of Education

Yoga is the practical path for 'Realization of Samkhya Philosophy'. Patanjali is founder of yoga system. Chitta Vrithi Nirodha is opening yoga sutra. Chitta means functional mind. Vrithi means whirlpool. Nirotha means silencing. Hence, it means, 'Silencing of the fluctuating state of the mind'. Yoga advocates 'Control over the body, the senses and the mind'. Sensual attachment and passions distract the body as well as the mind. To overcome this 'Astanga Yoga' needed Ex. Eightfold-path.

- Yama-Ahimsa and satya
- Niyama-Practice of tolerance external and internal cleanliness
- Asana- Steady and comfortable postures for meditation
- Pranayama-Inhalation, retention and exhalation
- Pratyahara- With drawings the senses from objects.
- Dharana-Fixing mind on object of meditation
- Dhyana-When the knowledge of object continued
- Samathi-Identified the objects of meditation

Brihadisvara Temple, Thanjavur District, Tamilnadu
Photograph - **Dr. N. Anandakumar**

E. Purva MimamsaPhilosophy of Education

Mimamsa means enquiry or investigation. It is 'Revealed thought process'. Its emphases 'Ritualistic aspect of the Vedas (Karma Mimamsa). Jaimini is the founder of Mimamsa. Mimamsa accepts maximum Pramanas.

1. Perception (Pratyaksa)
2. Inference (Anumana)
3. Comparison (Upamana)
4. Verbal testimony (Sabda)
5. Postulation (Arthapati)
6. Non-apprehension (Anupalabhti)

Dharma is considered as the 'Highest Purushartha' in Mimamsa philosophy. Dharma arises from Karma (Action). There are two good Karmas:

1. Kamya Karma (Sacrificial Actions)
2. Nitya Karma (Daily Performed Actions)

Earlier portion of the Vedas is Purva Mimamsa. Purva Mimamsa is 'To interpret and establish the authority of Vedas'.

F. Uttara Mimamsa Philosophy of Education

It gives more importance to the knowledge aspect of the Vedas (Jnana Mimamsa-Vedanta). Vedanta literally means, the end of the Veda. Vedanta widened to include all thoughts developed out of the Upanishads. Commentaries of Brahmasutra, are more relevant to the study of Vedanta.

Vedanta have the individual self (Atman) and the cosmic self (Brahman).For example:

A. According to Sankaracharya, Atman and Brahman are not two different entities (Non-dualism). Brahman alone is real. Material world is an illusion. Atman is not different from Brahman. Sankaracharya talks three levels of existence.

1. Phenomenal Existence
2. Empirical Existence
3. Absolute Existence.

All practical purposes, the world is to be considered as real but it is not absolutely real. The world of experience as indefinable. Maya hides the real Brahman and project the unreal world.

B. According to Ramanujacharya two entities are related together as part and whole. (Qualified monism) called Visistadvaita. Visista-Advaita emphasis 'Supreme being has a definite form'. Ex. Vishnu possesses attributes. Brahman (God) and Atman (Soul) is identical in some aspects. All knowledge involves distinctions but, there is no undifferentiated pure consciousness. Brahman is qualified.

C. According to Madhvacharya, two entities are totally different (Dualism). Dvaita says that different is the reality. Atman and Brahman are different and independent. There are not one but two. Ex. God and Soul.

BUDDHISM PHILOSOPHY OF EDUCATION

Introduction to Buddhism Philosophy

Buddhism developed as a distinct system in the 6th century B.C. It was founded by Guatama Buddha. He was born in 563-483 B.C at Lumbini of Kapilavastu Nagar, Nepal. He was primarily an ethical teacher and social reformer. He repeatedly told, "Human existence is full of misery and pain". Buddhism written in Pali. These works are based Tri-Pitaka (Teaching of Buddha).

1. Sutta pitaka (Utterances of Buddha's Doctrines and ethics)
2. Vinaya pitaka (Rules of Discipline)
3. Abhidhammapitaka (Philosophical discussion)

Pitaka in Pali language means 'Basket'. Teaching of Buddha is threefold:

1. Four noble truths
2. Noble eight-fold path
3. Doctrine of dependent origination.

Aryasatya means noble truth. In Sanskrit 'Chatvariaryasatyani'.

1. There is suffering (Dukkha)
2. Cause for suffering (Dukkha hetu or karana)
3. Cessation of suffering (Dukka nirodha)
4. There is a way leading to the removal of suffering (Dukkha nirodhamarga).

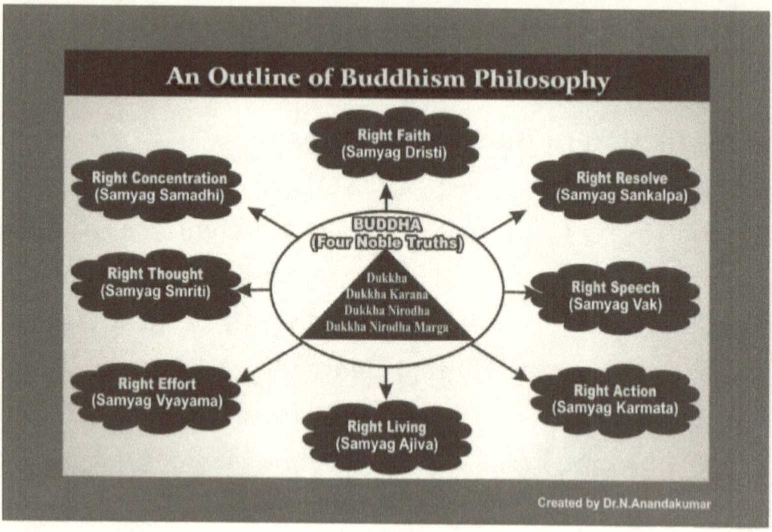

Figure: 2 Shows an outline of Buddhism philosophy.

As compared to Vedic philosophy, Buddhist education system was not rigid in rituals. 200BC to 200AD Buddhist education system has developed. Teaching of Buddha

1. All things are conditional nature.
2. Neither any soul nor God or any other permanent substances.
3. Everything is change process.
4. Tree generates another tree through the seed.

Buddha offered to impart education to all. They recommend education start at age of eight 'Shramana' till the age of 12. Qualified to become monk at the age of 20. Pali was the medium of instruction. A ritual called as 'Pabbaja Ritual' was admission to a monastery to education (Students called Shramana).

Features of rituals:

1. One had to get his head shaved wear yellow clothes
2. Sit cross-legged
3. One was then repeated the sentences
    a. I take refuge to Buddha
    b. I take refuge to Iteema
    c. I take refuge to Sangha

One was required to obey the following center rules-Abstain from:

a. Theft, killing of any living beings
b. Impure conduct
c. Use of intoxicating things
d. Use of cosmetics
e. Taking things without being offered
f. Accepting objects of gold and silver in alms
g. Watching dance and listening of music

Upsamapada Rituals:

Upsamapada rituals performed at the age of 20. Male monks were now called as Bikshe and female as Bikshuni.

Contribution of Buddhist Education:

a. General education a significant position
b. Respect developed for manual and practical skills

Aims of Education:

a. Teaching of Buddha
b. Development of personality
c. Nirvana

Buddha institutions:

a. Taxilla University: Taxilla was the Capital of Gandhara (Taxa, the son of the King Bharata).
b. Nalanta University: The University was situated in Bihar.
c. Ballabhi University: A famous center of Buddhism (475AD to 775 AD in Kathiavar)
d. Vikramshila University: Situated in Banks of Ganga, Magadha, Bihar. Tibetan language used.
e. Mithila and Nadia Universities: They used logic study.

Philosophical Ideas of Buddhism:

Change is ultimate reality. Everything is momentary. There is no soul. All have transient sensations. Every effect has a cause. His theory of 'Pratityasamutpada' (Dependent origination) explains the root cause of suffering in the form of a causal wheel variously called Bhava chakra, Samsara Chakra and Jara-marana Chakra. The causal wheel contains 12 spokes:

1. Ignorance (Avidya)
2. Action (Samskara)
3. Consciousness (Vjnana)
4. Name and form (Nama-rupa)
5. Mind- Sense organs (Sadayatana)
6. Sense object contact (Sparsha)
7. Sense experience (Vedana)
8. Thirst for sense enjoyment (Trsna)
9. Clinging to existence (Upadana)

10. Being (Bhava)
11. Re-birth (Jati)
12. Old age and death (Jara-marana)

Everything in this world arises 'depending on the cause' (Impermanent). Buddha believes that suffering, which resulted due to ignorance led to the endless cycle of births and deaths.

He considered that knowledge is the chief meansof reformation,individual and society. Taking pragmatic view "Usefulness is the criterion for right knowledge" Two Pramanas: Pratyaksa (Perception) and Annumana (Inference).

It is moralistic nature. Its central theme is "Finding a solution for cause". The four noble truths and Ashtanga Marga (eight-fold path) comprise 'Buddha ethics. These truths discuss the path self-discipline which leads man to liberation (Nirvana). Buddha's eight-fold path (Ashtanga Marga) to nirvana comprises. This eightfold path can be attained only after the previous steps.

JAINISM PHILOSOPHY OF EDUCATION

Introduction to Jainism Philosophy

The Jainas, the names of twenty-four teachers believed to have come down from 'Unknown antiquity'. The first of these teachers was Rishabhadeva. The last was Vardhamana. They lived in the sixth century B.C., during the time of Gotama Buddha. The word Jina etymologically means a conqueror. They have conquered all passions and have attained liberation.

The Jainas do not believe in God. The Jainas believe that every spirit (Jiva), that is in bondage now, can follow the example set by the Jainas and attain, like them, perfect knowledge, perfectpower and perfectjoy. Jainism possesses a vast literature, mostly in Prakrta.

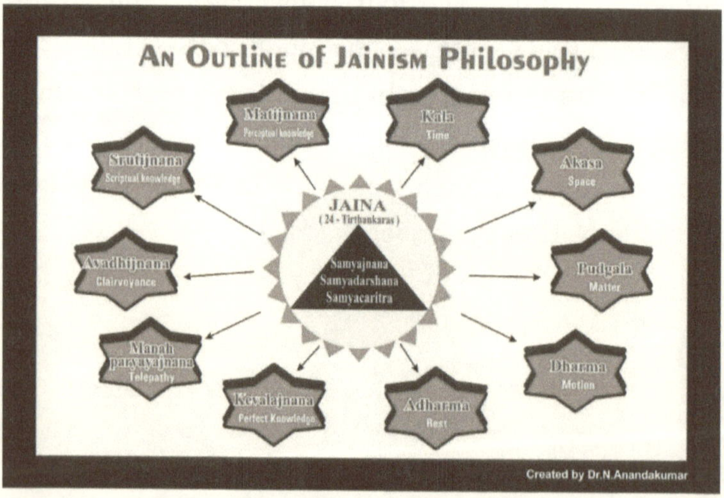

Figure: 3 Shows an outline of Jainism philosophy

The philosophical outlook of Jainism is 'Common-sense realism' and pluralism. The objects perceived byreal, and many. Every living being has a spirit or a soul (Jiva). Avoidance of all injury to life, an important role in Jaina ethics. Metaphysical theory of reality as many-faced (Anekantavada) and a consequent logical doctrine (Syadvada).

Jainism believes in the reality of the external objective world like realism

The reality is Dravya or substance. It has two forms:

a. Essential
b. Accidental

Universe into two categories:

a. Jivas (Souls-consciousness)
b. Ajivas (Non-souls-non-consciousness)

Ajiva has five categories:

a. Kala (Time)
b. Akasa (Space)
c. Pudgala (Matter)
d. Dharma (Motion)
e. Adharma (Rest)

Human knowledge is finite and cannot comprehend them. Jaina is relativistic nature. There are innumerable material atoms and souls. Matter and spirit are independent realities. All our judgements can never be absolutely affirmative (Negative) but only relative. Gandhiji says "It is the great lesson of tolerance".

Jaina logic distinguishes seven forms of judgements:

1. Syadasti (May be it is)
2. Syadnasti (May be it is not)
3. Syadastinasti (May be it is and it is not)
4. Syadavaktavyah (May be it is indescribable)
5. Syadasticaavaktavyah (May it is and is indescribable)
6. Syadnasticaavaktavyah (May it is not and is indescribable)
7. Syadasticanasticaavaktavyah (May be it is, is not and is indescribable)

Shravanabelagola, Hassan District, Karnataka State
Photograph - **Dr. N. Anandakumar**

Jainism classified five different forms of knowledge:

1. Matijnana (Perceptual knowledge)
2. Srutijnana (Scriptural knowledge)
3. Avadhijnana (Clairvoyance)
4. Manahparyayajnana (Telepathy)
5. Kevalajnana (Perfect knowledge)

Jain Pramanas:

a. Perception
b. Inference
c. Verbal testimony

It is atheistic religion, preaching moral code. Moral path to liberation is based three precious principles called Tri-Ratnas (three gems).

1. Samya-jnana (Right knowledge)
2. Samya-darshana (Right faith)
3. Samya-caritra (Right conduct)

Ignorance is the real cause of bondage. It can be removed only by right knowledge.

There are five great vows under the practical discipline.

a. Non-injury (Ahimsa)
b. Non-uttering of falsehood (Satya)
c. Non-stealing (Asteya)
d. Abstention from self-indulgence (Brahmachariya)
e. Non-possession (Aparigraha)

Jainism is a religionwithout God, but spiritualistic and ethical nature. It denies God, it accepts Godhead.

Sittanavasal, Pudukkottai District, Tamil Nadu
Photograph - **Dr. N. Anandakumar**

Educational Implications of Jainism

1. Self-realization: Jainism believes personality development and self-development. The individual and social aspects of personality are equally emphasized. Man's soul is more important rather than his material. Self-realization is to enable the child to realize their soul.
2. Preservation of culture: It emphasizes culture environments rather than materials.
3. Development of Moral Sense: It enables him to distinguish right from wrong, to love good and despise evil.
4. Simple living: Jainism regards that simple living and high thinking should be another aim of education.
5. Development of complete Man: It means, physically he must be stout, intellectually, he must be alert and think like a philosopher and scientist, morally he should have determination to follow good and to avoid evil, spiritually he should have the freedom of mind, freedom from ignorance, wants and passions.

REFERENCES

1. Aggarwal, J.C. (2000). Theory and Principles of Education-Philosophical and Sociological Bases of Education. *Vikas Publishing House (P) Ltd., Delhi-32,* 42-53.
2. Aggarwal, J.C. (2011). Teacher and Education in a Developing Society. *Vikas Publishing House (P) Ltd., Noida,* 24-38.
3. Banerjee, A.C., & Sharma, S.R. (1999). Sociological and Philosophical Issues in Education. *Book Enclave, Jaipur, India,* 153-212.
4. Barrow, Rabin., & Woods, Ronald. (2006). An Introduction to Philosophy of Education, 4th, Edition. *Routledge, Taylor & Francis Group, London,* 01-06.
5. Bhatt, Siddheshwar Rameshwar. (2018). Philosophical Foundations of Educations-Lessons for Indian. *Springer Nature, Singapore (P) Ltd., Singapore,* 01-15.
6. Chand, Jagdish. (2010). Philosophical Foundations of Education. *Anshah Publishing House, Delhi-92,* 124-148.
7. Chandra, S.S., & Sharma, R.K. (2007). Philosophy of Education. *Atlantic Publishers & Distributors (P) Ltd., New Delhi-27,* 32-40.
8. Chaube, S.P., & Chaube, A. (2009). Foundations of Education. *Vikas Publishing House (P) Ltd., Noida,* 77-91.

9. Dunn, Sheila, G. (2005). Philosophical Foundations of Education-Connecting Philosophy to Theory and Practices, *Pearson Education, New Jersey,* 01-12.
10. Fernandes, Maria Meleagris. (2004). The Foundations of Education: The Philosophical Approach. *Himalaya Publishing House, Mumbai,* 53-68.
11. Ganguly, M., Srivastava, G., Gupta, V., Rajaram., K., & Ramamurthy, V. (2010). Facets of Indian Culture. *Spectrum Books (P) Ltd., New Delhi-58,* 16-49.
12. Gutek, Gerald L. (2004). Philosophical and Ideological Voices in Education. *Pearson Education, Boston, MA,* 107-119.
13. Goswami, Dulumoni. (2013). Philosophy of Education. *DVS Publishers, Guwahati-01,* 01-19.
14. Heyting, Frieda., Lenzen, Dieter., & White, John. (2002). Methods in Philosophy of Education. *Routledge, Taylor & Francis Group, London,* 01-12.
15. Khanna, S.D., Saxena, V.K., Lamba, T.P., & Murthy, V. (2010). Education in the Emerging Indian Society. *DOABA House, Booksellers & Publishers, Delhi-6,* 44-50.
16. Khan, Wasim Ahmad. (2011). Philosophical Foundation of Education. *Lakshay Publication, New Delhi-02,* 67-87.
17. Lakshmanan, K. (2013). Indian Philosophy (Tamil Edition). *Palaniappa Brothers, Tiruchirappalli,* 09-67.
18. Mohanty, Jagannath. (2011). Dynamics of Educational Thoughts and Practices. *Shipra Publications, New Delhi-02,* 104-109.

19. Moore, T.W. (2010). Philosophy of Education: An Introduction. *Routledge & Kegan Paul, Taylor & Francis, London,* 01-08.
20. Moore, Brooke Noel., & Bruder, Kenneth. (2011). Philosophy-The Power of Ideas-8th, Edition. *Tata McGraw Hill Education (P) Ltd., New Delhi,* 13-15.
21. Seetharamu, A.S. (2004). Philosophies of Education. *Ashish Publishing House, New Delhi-26,* 01-10.
22. Sharma. (2002). Philosophical and Sociological Foundations of Education. *Lakshmi Narain Agarwal, Agra-3,* 01.25.
23. Thamarasseri, Ismail. (2008). Education in the Emerging Indian Society. *Kanishka Publishers & Distributors, New Delhi,* 26-58.
24. Veeraiah, B. (2003). Education in Emerging India. *Himalaya Publishing House, Mumbai,* 41-100.

www.ingramcontent.com/pod-product-compliance
Lightning Source LLC
Chambersburg PA
CBHW050026170726
48282CB00025B/569
* 9 7 8 9 3 9 1 3 7 3 6 8 9 *